INSPIRATIONAL SHORT SOCCER STORIES FOR YOUNG RISING ACHIEVERS

THE INCREDIBLE JOURNEY OF 15 SOCCER
CHAMPIONS, DESIGNED TO INSPIRE AND CAPTIVATE
THE HEARTS OF YOUNG SOCCER FANS AND ASPIRING
ATHLETES WORLDWIDE

ELVIN CREATIONS

CONTENTS

INTRODUCTION

Soccer transcends its status as a sport and becomes a symphony of talent, emotion, and unwavering spirit in the enchanted world where the clamor of the audience meets the balletic movement of the ball. Welcome to "Legends of the Beautiful Game: Tales of Soccer's Finest," a journey through time that retells the incredible stories of people whose footsteps on the field have resonated down the years.

Soccer is a worldwide language that reaches to the hearts of millions of people. We dig into the lives and careers of the most memorable people that have graced the pitch in this anthology of excellence. From Pelé's majestic creativity to Messi and Ronaldo's ethereal brilliance, each episode unveils a narrative of unmatched commitment, astounding skill, and the quest of perfection that transcends boundaries.

As the globe comes together in its passion for this wonderful game, we ask readers of all ages to delve into the stories that have woven soccer into the fabric of our collective consciousness. Beyond the spectacular goals and tremendous applause, these stories capture the essence of tenacity, collaboration, and the unwavering pursuit of aspirations.

This book is a treasure mine of inspiration for both young fans anxious to put on their cleats and seasoned supporters reminiscing about the golden days. The stories in these pages are about more than simply goals; they are about fights won, hurdles conquered, and the unbreakable spirit that distinguishes soccer's genuine legends.

Join us as we travel through the highs and lows, victories and hardships, and see how these players engraved their names in the pantheon of soccer glory by pure will and skill. "Legends of the Beautiful Game" is more than simply a compilation of stories; it's an invitation to experience the enchantment, perspiration, and indomitable spirit that make soccer more than just a game, but a way of life. Prepare to be intrigued by the stories of soccer's greatest players, where the pitch transforms into a canvas and each player becomes an artist, creating memories that will last forever.

1

PELE

"Success is no accident. It is hard work, perseverance, learning, studying, sacrifice, and most of all, love of what you are doing or learning to do."

A kid named Edson Arantes do Nascimento took his first steps in the sun-kissed streets of Três Coraçes, Brazil, where dreams were as plentiful as the palm palms lined the horizon. Little did the world realize that from these humble beginnings would emerge a football prodigy, a worldwide legend destined to rewrite the story of the beautiful game - Pelé.

THE PASSION SEED:

Pelé's childhood was marked by a strong bond with the ball, since he was born on October 23, 1940. Growing up in poverty, Edson's playground was the dusty streets of Bauru, and his first love was a rag-made ball. The rhythmic echo of bare feet on difficult ground signaled the start of a journey that would see a shoeless youngster become a symbol of footballing greatness.

Santos FC's Discovery and Journey:

Pelé's fortuitous meeting with coach Waldemar de Brito was the impetus that catapulted him from the dusty streets to the pinnacle of professional football. Recognizing Pelé's natural aptitude, de Brito sponsored his transfer to the Santos Football Club at the age of 15. It was here that the world saw the raw brilliance that would define Pelé's legacy for the first time.

Pelé made his debut with Santos in 1956, kicking off a stratospheric climb. Santos' spectacular talents, bold goals, and instinctive grasp of the game elevated him to the status of a juggernaut, catching the minds of fans all across Brazil. A celebrity was created when Pelé danced past defenders, and his trajectory would soon transcend beyond national lines.

The World Stage's Precocious Prodigy:

The 17-year-old star made his international debut in the 1958 World Cup in Sweden. Pelé, dressed in the classic yellow jersey, had a style that combined grace and daring. Pelé led Brazil to its first World Cup triumph in a campaign defined by magnificent goals and exceptional skill, becoming the youngest player to score in a World Cup final.

Pelé's unrivaled supremacy continued in the years that followed. His duets with Santos became legendary, and his international reputation skyrocketed. Pelé was already a force to be reckoned with by the time the 1962 World Cup arrived. However, a tragic twist of fate forced him to miss time due to injury, leading admirers to speculate on what may have been.

The 1970 World Cup was the pinnacle of success.

If Pelé's 1958 victory launched him into the world stage, the 1970 World Cup in Mexico was the pinnacle of his career. Pelé, now a three-time Ballon d'Or winner, led a star-studded Brazilian squad on a captivating trip at the age of 29.

The final vs Italy is in football legend. Pelé's header in the 18th minute and magnificent assist for Carlos Alberto's goal summed up his brilliance. Brazil triumphed, and Pelé set an incredible record by winning three World Cups—a record that stands to this day.

Beyond the Goals: Pelé, the Football Gentleman:

While Pelé's goal-scoring exploits are legendary, his effect goes beyond numbers. Pelé was a symbol of change at an era when sportsmen were rarely active about cultural concerns. In the middle of Brazil's volatile political scene, he utilized his position to call for social justice, peace, and equality.

Pelé's dedication to fair play and sportsmanship also distinguished him. He was known for his dislike of accepting penalties and liked to win through talent and collaboration rather than the easy way. His humility off the field, along with his dogged pursuit of success on it, won him followers all over the world.

Legacy After the Last Whistle:

As the last whistle sounded on Pelé's spectacular career, his legacy evolved. Beyond the pitch, he remained a global football ambassador, championing the sport's unifying potential. His humanitarian activities, notably those to UNICEF, demonstrate a man whose heart reached well beyond the pitch.

Injuries may have limited Pelé's playing career, but they could not lessen his legacy. Pelé, the once-barefooted youngster with ambitions as big as the Brazilian horizon, is now an everlasting legend, a tribute to the transformational power of sport and the tenacity of a great champion.

WHAT DID WE LEARN FROM HIM ?

Pelé, a legendary personality in the world of football, delivers priceless teachings that transcend athletics, embodying attributes and concepts applicable to life's greater canvas. At the center of his story is an unbreakable spirit of passion and determination. Pelé's constant passion for football, seen from his early kickabouts on the slums of Bauru to the grandeur of World Cup stadiums, reminds us the transformational power of true excitement.

His rise from obscurity to global acclaim is a striking tribute to the value of hard work and determination. Pelé's dedication to developing his abilities and overcoming obstacles demonstrates that success is won by hard work and an unwavering pursuit of perfection, not just talent.

Pelé's attitude to the game exemplifies the value of cooperation and sportsmanship. His resistance to taking penalties, preferring triumphs achieved by talent and teamwork, emphasizes the importance of fair play and togetherness. Beyond the field, Pelé's support for social justice and humanitarian causes demonstrates the influence that people may have on larger societal concerns.

The Brazilian legend's tenacity in the face of adversity, from surviving injuries to rebounding from defeats, teaches us how to confront life's problems with unyielding resolve. Pelé's attitude of embracing problems as chances for personal and communal progress supports embracing challenges not as obstacles but as possibilities for personal and collective improvement.

"The more difficult the victory, the greater the happiness in winning."

2

ALFREDO DI STEFANO

"When you win, you don't get carried away. But if you go step by step, with confidence, you can go far."

Few names in football history evoke the same symphony of skill, flexibility, and leadership as Alfredo Di Stéfano. Di Stéfano was born in Buenos Aires, Argentina, on July 4, 1926, and went on to become not just one of the finest footballers of his age, but also a master whose impact reached well beyond the game.

EARLY YEARS: THE BIRTH OF A FOOTBALL PRODIGY

Di Stéfano's adventure began on the streets of Buenos Aires, where he shown an instinctive knack for the beautiful game. His boyhood, on the other hand, was far from ideal. Di Stéfano's early years were marred by financial challenges that shaped his endurance and determination as he grew up amid a period of economic turbulence.

Despite the difficulties, Di Stéfano's extraordinary skill was clear from an early age. He joined River Plate's youth divisions, one of Argentina's most historic teams, and swiftly advanced through the ranks. His skill, vision, and adaptability set him unique, capturing the attention of both football fans and pros.

The Colombian Odyssey: Millonarios' Unprecedented Success

In the early 1950s, a unique chapter in Di Stéfano's career developed, cementing his place as a global footballing superstar. Di Stéfano ended himself in Colombia after a conflict between local football officials in Argentina. He signed with Millonarios. This unexpected change of events signaled the start of a remarkable period for both the athlete and the organization.

Di Stéfano had a profound effect on Colombian football. He guided Millonarios to four consecutive league titles, demonstrating his capacity to not only adapt to but also elevate a new footballing culture. His leadership abilities and devotion to greatness set the foundation for Millonarios' golden period.

Real Madrid's Dynasty: European Glory Calls

The footballing world was calling Di Stéfano, and he joined Real Madrid in 1953, a club that would become synonymous with his reputation. His arrival signaled the start of a dazzling chapter in Real Madrid's history, converting the club into a European powerhouse.

Real Madrid won five consecutive European Cups under Di Stéfano's captaincy and influence from 1956 to 1960, an unprecedented accomplishment in the competition's history. Di Stéfano's style of play was revolutionary—he flawlessly melded elegance, strength, and intellect, confounding opponents and enchanting fans.

Versatility and Vision: The Maestro's Toolbox

Di Stéfano's greatness stemmed not just from his technical prowess but also from his unrivaled adaptability. He could play as a striker, midfielder, or even a defender, adjusting his style to the demands of the club. On the field, his vision was comparable to that of a chess genius, organizing attacks with an inherent awareness of space and timing.

This versatility and football savvy were on full show against AC Milan in the 1958 European Cup final. Di Stéfano, who is known for his goal-scoring prowess, took on the role of facilitator, setting up all four goals in Real Madrid's 4-3 triumph, demonstrating his versatility.

The Will to Win in the Face of Difficulties

Di Stéfano's trip was not without its difficulties. A heartbreaking defeat to Benfica in the European Cup final in 1962 was a rare moment of despair. However,

Di Stéfano bounced back, guiding Real Madrid to further domestic and international glory in the years that followed.

Di Stéfano's final appearance in the European Cup would come against Inter Milan in 1964. While he did not win that game, his status as a pioneering force in football was assured. His influence stretched beyond the field, as he inspired a generation of footballers and left an indelible stamp on the Real Madrid style of play.

Beyond Club Allegiances, a Global Icon

Di Stéfano's influence extended beyond the club arena. His international career, on the other hand, was defined by the intricacies of national team loyalty. Di Stéfano never played for Argentina in the World Cup due to football's regulatory organizations at the time. Nonetheless, his influence extended well beyond the confines of international tournaments.

Di Stéfano later represented three national teams in unofficial friendlies: Argentina, Colombia, and Spain, in an act of football diplomacy. This one-of-a-kind honor underscored his ability to bridge borders, uniting followers from all around the world under the flag of his extraordinary footballing genius.

The Elder Statesman: Leadership for a New Generation

As his playing days came to an end, Di Stéfano moved easily into coaching and administration, becoming a knowledgeable elder statesman of the game. His thoughts and leadership created a new generation of players, and his affiliation with Real Madrid lasted in numerous positions, cementing his place in the club's history as an everlasting figure.

WHAT DID WE LEARN FROM HIM?

Alfredo Di Stéfano, a footballing legend, teaches deep lessons throughout his illustrious career. His agility, fluidly switching between postures, reminds us the importance of adaptation in dealing with life's obstacles. Di Stéfano's vision on the pitch, directing assaults with precision, demonstrates the value of foresight and strategic thought in sports and in life.

The Argentine's persistence is seen in his ability to overcome losses, like as the 1962 European Cup final loss, indicating that failures are not defeats but rather stepping stones to future successes. Di Stéfano's influence goes beyond boundaries, as he has represented numerous national teams in unofficial friendlies, highlighting the unifying power of sports across cultures.

Di Stéfano's mentorship as a coach and administrator highlights the obligation of seasoned persons to advise and encourage the next generation. His faith in football's fundamental principles, which transcend tactical changes, teaches a timeless lesson in the lasting qualities of discipline and determination.

Alfredo Di Stéfano's legacy, in essence, rings with the attributes of flexibility, vision, resilience, unity, mentoring, and eternal values—a monument to the deep influence a sports great can have on influencing not just the beautiful game but also the character of those who follow in his footsteps.

"In football as in watchmaking, talent and elegance mean nothing without rigour and precision."

3

LIONEL MESSI

"There are more important things in life than winning or losing a game."

LIONEL MESSI'S JOURNEY FROM ROSARIO TO GLORY: A STORY OF MAGICAL FEET AND A UNYIELDING SPIRIT

A legend was formed in the calm neighborhoods of Rosario, Argentina, where the noises of children playing football resound through the air. Lionel Messi, born on June 24, 1987, would rise from humble beginnings to become one of the world's best footballers. This is the inspiring story of a little child who has a ball, a dream, and the determination to overcome the hurdles set against him.

The Light in Rosario

Rosario, a city famed for its love of football, was the ideal home for Lionel Messi's remarkable potential. Messi showed an intuitive affinity with the ball as a child, dribbling through homemade goalposts in his neighborhood's tiny alleyways. His small height did not discourage him; rather, it created the foundation of his evasive and captivating playing style.

Messi's early years were highlighted by the difficulties of being from a low-income family. His family was struggling financially, and little Lionel was diagnosed with a growth hormone deficit. Nonetheless, hardship would prove to be the furnace in which Messi's unbreakable character was created.

The Trip to Barcelona

Messi's life was transformed when he joined FC Barcelona's youth divisions at the age of 13. His brilliance, obvious even in his early years, drew the attention of the football world. His migration to Barcelona, away from his family in Argentina, was a tribute to the sacrifices that must be made in order to achieve a goal.

Messi's new playground became Barcelona, where his amazing gifts were nurtured at the legendary La Masia academy. Messi's growth surge, along with his spectacular skills, began to alter the possibilities of football under the mentoring of coaches who recognized his potential.

The Ascension of the "Flea"

Messi debuted for Barcelona as a 16-year-old, wearing the famed number 30 shirt. The football world was about to witness a phenomenon. Messi's rapid bursts of speed, unmatched ball control, and knack for goal-scoring earned him the nickname "La Pulga" (The Flea).

Messi became a regular starter in the 2005-2006 season, establishing a deadly combination alongside Ronaldinho and Samuel Eto'o. Barcelona's style, known as "tiki-taka," became synonymous with their success, and Messi was the central figure in this hypnotic footballing symphony.

The Triple Victory

The 2008-2009 season was a watershed moment in Messi's career. Barcelona won a historic triple under Pep Guardiola, winning La Liga, the Copa del Rey, and the UEFA Champions League. Messi's performance was critical; his 38 goals across all competitions demonstrated an individual brilliance that few could equal.

The sight of Messi gliding past defenders, leaving them in his wake, became the season's defining theme. His ability to break down defenses and score from almost impossible positions propelled him to the pinnacle of football aristocracy.

The Glorious Years

Messi's star continued to soar in the years that followed. He won many Ballon d'Or honors, solidifying his position as the finest player on the globe. His midfield connection with Xavi Hernandez and Andrés Iniesta in Barcelona became legendary, revolutionizing what a football club could do in terms of creativity and success.

Messi's scoring records fell like dominoes. His left foot transformed into a wand capable of conjuring magic at command, and his comprehension of the game reached a level of complexity bordering on clairvoyant. Each game was a canvas, and Messi was the artist with the magical brush.

The International Quest for the Unfinished Symphony

While Messi's domestic success with Barcelona was unsurpassed, an elusive goal remained on the international stage: the FIFA World Cup. As Argentina's representative, Messi faced high expectations and comparisons to the country's footballing great, Diego Maradona.

Messi led Argentina to the World Cup final in Brazil in 2014. Despite his outstanding exploits, which included four goals and multiple assists, Argentina was defeated in the final by Germany. Messi's resolve to achieve on the greatest stage of them all was motivated by the anguish of coming so close.

Redemption and Copa America Victory

Messi's path hit a turning point in the 2021 Copa America. Messi led Argentina to triumph in the tournament staged in Brazil after years of near misses and heartbreaks with the national squad. The sight of Messi raising the trophy, tears flowing down his cheeks, summed years of hard work and the realization of a lifelong desire.

Legacy Aside from Football

Beyond his spectacular goals and countless honors, Messi's legacy includes resilience, humility, and generosity. His personal battles with growth hormone insufficiency were a source of motivation for many others suffering similar difficulties. The Leo Messi Foundation, founded in 2007, displays his dedication to delivering healthcare and education to underprivileged youngsters.

WHAT DID WE LEARN FROM HIM?

Lionel Messi teaches us priceless lessons via his incredible journey from the streets of Rosario to become a global football hero. His unshakable dedication to his goals, fuelled by sacrifice and unflinching hard work, embodies the spirit of perseverance and tenacity. Messi's narrative motivates us to see obstacles as chances for growth and to endure in the face of hardship.

Messi's emphasis on collaboration and selflessness, in addition to his unrivaled brilliance on the field, reminds us that genuine success is attained together. His preference for team titles above individual prizes emphasizes the value of teamwork and shared successes. Messi's dedication to continual growth inspires us to never settle for mediocrity and to constantly explore methods to better our skills and abilities.

Furthermore, Messi's humility and focus on becoming a nice person first and foremost before being a football player illustrate the value of character and integrity in the pursuit of success. He teaches us that there are more important things in life than winning or losing a game. Messi's career shows the transformative power of passion, hard work, humility, and a balanced outlook —a legacy that extends well beyond the football field.

"You have to fight to reach your dream. You have to sacrifice and work hard for it."

4

CRISTIANO RONALDO

"Dreams are not what you see in your sleep, dreams are things which do not let you sleep."

CRISTIANO RONALDO: A JOURNEY FROM MADEIRA TO IMMORTALITY

In the sun-kissed island of Madeira, Portugal, on February 5, 1985, a star was born. Cristiano Ronaldo dos Santos Aveiro entered the world with a fervor that would one day shake the foundations of football. From humble beginnings to global stardom, Ronaldo's journey is not just the story of a footballer but a testament to unyielding determination, unparalleled work ethic, and an insatiable hunger for greatness.

The Island of Dreams

Born into a working-class family, Ronaldo's childhood in Madeira was marked by modest means. His father, a kit man at a local football club, ignited the spark that would set young Cristiano on a trajectory toward greatness. From improvised games in the narrow streets to showcasing his raw talent at Andorinha, his first club, Ronaldo's prodigious skill became impossible to ignore.

Sporting CP - The Launchpad

At the tender age of 12, Ronaldo left Madeira to join the Sporting CP youth academy in Lisbon. This move marked the first seismic shift in his life, separating him from family and familiar surroundings. The academy became the crucible where Ronaldo's innate talent was honed, and his work ethic began to set him apart.

His performances with Sporting CP's senior team turned heads, and soon, the footballing powerhouse Manchester United came calling. In 2003, at the age of 18, Ronaldo made the leap to the English Premier League, leaving an indelible mark on Sporting CP and embarking on a journey that would shape football history.

Manchester United - Rise to Prominence

Ronaldo's arrival at Manchester United marked the beginning of an era. Under the tutelage of Sir Alex Ferguson, he transformed from a promising talent into a footballing phenomenon. His blend of skill, speed, and goal-scoring prowess dazzled fans. Ronaldo's work ethic was legendary; early morning training sessions and relentless dedication became his trademarks.

The 2007-2008 season was the pinnacle of Ronaldo's time at Manchester United. He led the club to a historic treble—Premier League, FA Cup, and UEFA Champions League. Individually, he secured the Ballon d'Or, cementing his status as the best player in the world. His journey from the streets of Madeira to the summit of European football was now etched in the annals of the sport.

Real Madrid - Galáctico Status

In 2009, Ronaldo made a blockbuster move to Real Madrid for what was then a world-record transfer fee. The weight of expectation was immense, but Ronaldo thrived under the spotlight. His goal-scoring exploits reached unprecedented levels. The Santiago Bernabéu became the theater where Ronaldo's brilliance unfolded.

The rivalry with Lionel Messi intensified as both players vied for the title of the world's best. Ronaldo's tenure at Real Madrid was marked by individual accolades, including four more Ballon d'Or awards. He led the club to four Champions League titles in five seasons, leaving an indelible mark as one of the greatest goal-scorers in the history of the competition.

Juventus - The Italian Sojourn

In 2018, Ronaldo embarked on a new challenge, joining Juventus in Serie A. His arrival signaled not just a new phase in his career but a testament to his relentless pursuit of excellence. Even in a new league, Ronaldo's goal-scoring exploits continued unabated, further solidifying his status as a global footballing icon.

International Glory - UEFA Euro 2016 and UEFA Nations League

While club success abounded, international glory remained an elusive quest for Ronaldo with the Portugal national team. However, in 2016, Portugal clinched the UEFA Euro Championship, with Ronaldo playing a pivotal role both on and off the pitch. His leadership and resilience shone through, despite an early injury in the final.

The UEFA Nations League triumph in 2019 added another international trophy to Ronaldo's illustrious career. His commitment to the national team showcased a different facet of his character—a leader willing to do whatever it takes for the collective success of his country.

Beyond Football - The Brand, The Philanthropist

Ronaldo's impact transcends the football pitch. His brand, CR7, is synonymous with excellence and success. From clothing lines to fragrances, Ronaldo's entrepreneurial spirit has transformed him into a global icon beyond the realm of sports.

His philanthropic endeavors further underscore his commitment to making a positive impact. From supporting children's hospitals to donating to disaster relief efforts, Ronaldo leverages his fame and fortune to contribute to society.

THE FITNESS FREAK - DISCIPLINE AND WORK ETHIC

Ronaldo's physical prowess is a result of an unparalleled work ethic. His dedication to fitness, diet, and recovery is a blueprint for aspiring athletes. Ronaldo's mantra is simple—talent alone is not enough; hard work and discipline are the keys to sustained success.

"Your love makes me strong, your hate makes me unstoppable."

5

ZINEDINE ZIDANE

"I have a need to play intensely every day, to fight every match hard."

ZINEDINE ZIDANE: ELEGANCE AND RESILIENCE MAESTRO

On June 23, 1972, a footballing talent was born in the tranquil neighbourhoods of La Castellane, a Marseille suburb. Zinedine Yazid Zidane, the son of Algerian immigrants, would go on to become one of the greatest midfielders and football idols of all time. This is Zizou's inspiring journey, a tale of grace, perseverance, and a career that unfolded like a painting on the canvas of the beautiful game.

The Beginning of a Footballing Odyssey

Growing up in Marseille's varied neighbourhoods, Zidane acquired his love for football among the sounds of youngsters playing in the streets. Smail, his father, spotted his son's promise early on and became his first coach, establishing discipline and a strong work ethic in him. Zidane's journey from La Castellane's harsh terrains to the huge stages of international football has begun.

The First Steps of AS Cannes

Zidane left his family's home at the age of 14 to attend AS Cannes' youth academy. The transformation was not only geographical, but also cultural, as Zidane navigated the issues of identification and belonging with his Algerian heritage. His experience at Cannes helped shape his football identity: a skilled, stylish player with a unique ability to manage the ball as if it were an extension of himself.

Girondins de Bordeaux: The Rising Star

Zidane's professional career began in 1992, when he joined Girondins de Bordeaux. He thrived under the tutelage of coach Rolland Courbis, displaying his playmaking ability and capturing the attention of football fans. In 1996, Zidane's efforts with Bordeaux earned him the Ligue 1 Player of the Year title, indicating his meteoric rise to popularity.

Juventus: The Crowning Glory of European Football

Zidane's career got him to Juventus, one of Europe's most prominent teams, in 1996. His presence in Turin coincided with the Bianconeri's reign of terror. Zidane had an instant impact, leading Juventus to Serie A crowns and successive UEFA Champions League finals. The 1997-1998 season concluded in a momentous moment when Zidane scored twice against Real

Madrid in the final, confirming Juventus' place at the pinnacle of European football.

World Cup 1998: The Birth of a National Hero

Zidane's international career reached its pinnacle in 1998, when France hosted the FIFA World Cup. The tournament served as Zidane's canvas, on which he created a masterpiece. France won the World Cup thanks to his two headers against Brazil in the final, and Zidane, with his trademark shaved head, became a national hero. The picture of him lifting the World Cup will live on in the minds of football fans all across the world.

Real Madrid's Galáctico Era Has Begun

The arrival of Zinedine Zidane to Real Madrid in 2001 signaled the beginning of the Galáctico era. Zidane took his talent to the Santiago Bernabéu, partnering with luminaries like as Luis Figo, Ronaldo Nazário, and Ral. Real Madrid's eighth European Cup was achieved with a volley in the 2002 UEFA Champions League final against Bayer Leverkusen, which is widely regarded as one of the greatest goals in football history.

The Headbutt: An Error in Timing

Zidane's remarkable career also has a blooper: the iconic headbutt in the 2006 FIFA World Cup final.

Zidane's fight with Marco Materazzi in his final professional match ruined his final performance on the great stage. While the episode was contentious, it does not eclipse the legacy of a player who, with his skill and grace, transcended the game.

The Coach and Mentor in Post-Retirement

Zidane's influence on football lasted far beyond his playing days. In his first year as a coach, he led Real Madrid to unparalleled success, including three straight UEFA Champions League wins from 2016 to 2018. Zidane's poise on the sidelines complemented his collected attitude on the field, and he became a role model for a new generation of sportsmen.

Elegance, Resilience, and Inspiration: Legacy

Zinedine Zidane's legacy is comprised not just of the trophies he won, but also of the grace with which he played the game. His ability to handle the ball, command the tempo, and deliver in vital situations distinguishes him. Zidane was more than a footballer; he was a maestro who orchestrated symphonies on the field.

Zidane's rise from the slums of La Castellane to the pinnacles of football is a monument to his fortitude. His Algerian ancestry, cultural struggles, and flaws fashioned him into an inspirational person. Zidane demonstrated that beauty and resilience can coexist, that little flaws do not define a career, and that greatness is defined not by winning but by how you play the game.

The Maestro's Coaching Symphony: Zinedine Zidane

Zinedine Zidane's transformation from iconic player to coaching guru added a new chapter to his football tale. He returned to Real Madrid in 2016, not as a player wearing the famous white shirt, but as the man in charge of leading the club through the turbulent seas of modern sport. What followed was a coaching voyage distinguished by exceptional success, strategic genius, and the calm temperament that he possessed throughout his playing days.

Real Madrid's Revenge

Zidane's coaching career began with Real Madrid, the most prominent club in the world. When he took over in January 2016, he inherited a squad full of talent but confronting issues. The hiring in the middle of the season aroused eyebrows, but Zidane's intimate awareness of the club's culture and the subtle dynamics of the dressing room proved crucial.

Champions League Victories: A Flying Start

Zidane's first season as a manager culminated in a fantastic achievement: winning the UEFA Champions League. Real Madrid's 2016 final victory over Atletico Madrid heralded the start of a historic streak. Three consecutive Champions League victories followed, an unprecedented record in contemporary sport. Real Madrid etched their names in the annals of footballing history thanks to Zidane's tactical knowledge and ability to extract the best from his players.

Success in La Liga: A Balancing Act

While Real Madrid's Champions League triumph was indisputable, Zidane drew criticism for Real Madrid's alleged disregard of local tournaments. Barcelona won La Liga in both the 2016-2017 and 2017-2018 seasons. However, Zidane's critics were silenced in the 2019-2020 season when he led Real Madrid to La Liga victory, demonstrating his versatility and mastery of several aspects of football administration.

The Galácticos and Man-Management

Navigating a group loaded with footballing superstars, the Galácticos, demands not just tactical brilliance but also good man-management. With his calm manner and thorough grasp of the players' mentality, Zidane achieved a balance that few have achieved. Cristiano

Ronaldo, Sergio Ramos, and Luka Modric flourished under his tutelage, demonstrating his ability to establish a peaceful and high-performing atmosphere.

The Mysteries of Zidane's Tactics

Zidane's teaching technique is a mystery, a synthesis of simplicity and efficacy. His strategy is based on pragmatism, adaptability, and a focus on exploiting opponents' vulnerabilities. Zidane's flexibility shone through whether he used a 4-3-3, 4-4-2, or a diamond formation. His focus on a strong defensive foundation combined with quick counter-attacks demonstrated a strategic mind that was always evolving.

Moments of Truth: The Subtle Touch

Zidane's selections in important times rang true with a slight touch that typified his coaching style. Zidane's interventions were calculated and successful, whether it was introducing a substitute whose impact proved decisive or making shrewd tactical alterations. His serene manner on the sidelines echoed the poised elegance that defined his playing days.

The Legacy and the Departure

With trademark elegance, Zidane announced his resignation from Real Madrid in May 2021. His decision highlighted the difficulties and expectations that come with being a football manager. Zidane established a legacy that extended beyond his playing accomplishments: an era of unrivaled success distinguished by an indomitable spirit and a dedication to greatness.

WHAT DID WE LEARN FROM HIM?

We learn from Zinedine Zidane that brilliance extends beyond the playing field—it's about orchestrating victory from the sidelines. As seen by his diverse tactical tactics, his coaching career teaches us the skill of flexibility. Zidane highlights the need of man-management in order to build unity among football players. His ability to maintain cool under pressure is demonstrated by his calm attitude in critical occasions. Zidane's legacy exemplifies the need of a deft touch in decision-making while leading teams to victory. Finally, he teaches that leadership is a dynamic blend of strategy, resilience, and the capacity to translate footballing aspirations into concrete results, leaving an unforgettable stamp on the coaching landscape of the beautiful game.

"The only way to win is as a team. Football is not about one or two or three star players."

6

FERENC PUSKAS

"Football is played with the head. Your feet are just the tools."

THE GALLOPING MAJOR'S SYMPHONY OF GOALS BY FERENC PUSKÁS

On April 1, 1927, a football prodigy was born in the little village of Kispest, Hungary. The world had no idea that this youngster, Ferenc Puskás, would grow up to become one of the greatest footballers of all time. His path, defined by stunning goals, tenacity, and an everlasting love for the beautiful game, would cement his name in football legend.

Early Childhood: A Child Playing with a Ball

Ferenc Puskás' love affair with football began in Kispest's unpaved streets. He had a natural aptitude from an early age, dribbling a ball with a flare that drew the attention of those around him. Ferenc was raised in a working-class household, but his enthusiasm for the sport propelled him well beyond his humble roots.

Kispest: Puskás's Brilliant Cradle

Puskás' skill grew at Kispest Honvéd, a small team that would serve as a blank canvas for his footballing genius.

His early efforts earned praise, and it wasn't long before he gained the attention of football fans outside of Hungary. The Galloping Major, as he became known afterward, was becoming a force to be reckoned with.

Honvéd and the Mighty Magyars: Hungarian Magic

Puskás' path paralleled a golden age in Hungarian football. He developed a strong team with talents such as Nándor Hidegkuti and Sándor Kocsis as a member of the Mighty Magyars. The team's offensive strategy highlighted Puskás' ability to score from any location on the field. Puskás' goals echoed well beyond Hungary's borders, and the Magical Magyars left an unforgettable impression.

Bern's Miracle: Heartbreak and Redemption

The 1954 World Cup Final in Bern, Switzerland, would be pivotal for Puskás. Hungary took on West Germany in what became known as the Miracle of Bern. Despite Puskás' early goal, Hungary was defeated 3-2. Puskás, who was injured, shown tenacity by playing through the discomfort. While the loss was painful, it spurred Puskás' resolve to reach new heights.

The Honvéd Exodus: A Journey to the International Stage

Political unrest in Hungary drove Puskás and other Honvéd players to seek sanctuary overseas. The migration signaled the start of Puskás' worldwide voyage. When he joined Real Madrid in 1958, he carried his goal-scoring ability to the glitzy stages of European football. The transfer catapulted Puskás to international prominence, and his effect at Real Madrid would be indelible.

The Maestro of Madrid: Goalscoring Extravaganza

Puskás had a very fantastic experience with Real Madrid. He carried the team to unparalleled success in a renowned combination with Alfredo Di Stéfano. Puskás' left foot unleashed a flurry of goals, and his ability to find the back of the net from unfathomable angles astounded observers. The Madrid Maestro, as he was popularly known, became synonymous with goal-scoring wizardry.

Puskás's Wembley Masterpiece: The Foggy Final

Puskás orchestrated a masterpiece in difficult circumstances in the 1960 European Cup Final at Wembley Stadium. In a 7-3 victory over Eintracht Frankfurt, he displayed his vision and skill while playing in dense fog. Puskás' performance is still regarded as one of the greatest individual displays in football history, cementing his place as a real maestro.

A Lasting Legacy: The Puskás Award

FIFA instituted the Puskás Award in 2009, an annual award awarded to the player who scored the year's most artistically noteworthy and beautiful goal. This honor recognizes Puskás's long-lasting influence on the sport. His legacy lives on not only in medals and statistics, but also in the creativity and delight he offered to football fans all across the world.

Conquering England and Beyond with the Golden Team

Puskás' reputation is inextricably linked to the successes of Hungary's Golden Team, the country's national team of the 1950s. Hungary played England at Wembley Stadium in 1953 in what became known as the Match of the Century. England, who had not lost at home in 90 years, was sure of victory. Puskás and the Golden Team, on the other hand, provided a footballing masterclass, thrashing England 6-3. Puskás' two goals demonstrated his genius, and the triumph marked a turning point in football history.

The Golden Team's success continued, and they were considered favorites to win the 1954 World Cup. Despite losing in the final, they had a significant effect on football's tactical growth. Puskás' impact extended beyond individual brilliance; he was the leader and spirit of a team that played with hitherto unheard beauty and refinement.

The Mentor and the Hungarian Hero in Post-Playing Days

Puskás' influence lasted well after his playing career. When he returned to Hungary, he began teaching and mentoring the next generation of footballers. His devotion to the sport and his country won him the honor of being named a national hero. Puskás' modesty and enthusiasm for the game allure him to fans, ensuring that his legacy lives on.

Real Madrid's Golden Era: Zidane in His Prime

Real Madrid began a golden era when Puskás delighted the Santiago Bernabéu with his creativity. The club dominated domestic and international competitions in the late 1950s and early 1960s. Puskás, dubbed the "Zidane of his generation," was in the vanguard of this triumph. Puskás' goals helped Real Madrid win multiple La Liga championships and European Cups during this period of dominance.

WHAT DID WE LEARN FROM HIM?

Ferenc Puskás teaches us about lasting talent, tenacity, and a deep passion for the beautiful game. His path tells us that talent, when fostered from humble origins, has the potential to transcend boundaries and enchant the world. Puskás' adaptability, as seen by his smooth transition from the streets of Kispest to the vast stages of international football, emphasizes the value of versatility and tenacity.

The Miracle of Bern, in which Puskás played through pain and heartache, teaches the importance of perseverance in the face of adversity. His contribution to Hungary's Golden Team, particularly its victory over England, teaches us about leadership and the power of collective genius. Puskás' transfer to Real Madrid, which launched the club's golden period, demonstrates the importance of individual greatness in team success.

Beyond the pitch, Puskás' post-playing position as a mentor and national hero exemplifies athletic idols' responsibilities to inspire and lead future generations. His long legacy, embodied in the Puskás Award, tells us that the creativity and delight he gave to football will be remembered for the rest of time. Ferenc Puskás, the Galloping Major, is more than a football icon; he is a source of inspiration, a witness to the transformational power of passion, talent, and unrelenting dedication to the game.

"Even when you are winning 3-0 or 4-0, you should not ease up. You should play the game in the same way you started it."

7

RONALDINHO GAUCHO

"God gives gifts to everyone, some can write, some can dance. He gave me the skill to play football and I am making the most of it."

RONALDINHO AND DESTINY: THE SAMBA MAGICIAN'S DANCE

Ronaldo de Assis Moreira, a little lad from the colorful streets of Porto Alegre, Brazil, was destined to become a football hero. Little did the world realize that this child, fondly known as Ronaldinho, would not only alter the beautiful game, but also dazzle millions with his magical abilities on the field.

Beginnings in Porto Alegre: The Dream Playground

Ronaldinho was born on March 21, 1980, in the underprivileged area of Vila Nova, where the rhythm of samba and the echoes of futsal bouncing off the streets shaped his early existence. Poverty engulfed him, yet the ball at his feet provided him unfathomable delight. Ronaldinho's distinct style, remarkable abilities, and contagious smile established him as a future prodigy.

Gremio's First Glimpse of Genius

Ronaldinho's path from the streets to the professional ranks began at Gremio. His senior debut revealed a skill that went beyond traditional limitations. The world witnessed the birth of a maestro, a player capable of making the ball dance to the beats of his mind.

A Brazilian in the City of Lights: Paris Saint-Germain

Ronaldinho left Brazil for the legendary Paris Saint-Germain in 2001. The birth of a footballing legend was seen in the City of Lights. Ronaldinho's performances were a carnival of skill, with his flicks and trickery perplexing opponents and awestruck fans. The magic he brought to the Parc des Princes offered relief to the PSG fans.

The Golden Years of the Barcelona Ballet

Ronaldinho's brilliance reached its pinnacle with FC Barcelona. He staged a balletic performance that would go down in football history, joined by players like Xavi and Andrés Iniesta. Ronaldinho's toothy grin became synonymous with the happy kind of football Barcelona played during his reign.

More Than a Player: The Joga Bonito Ambassador

Ronaldinho was more than simply a player; he was a representative of Joga Bonito—the beautiful game. His technique crossed national lines, and his smile became an international emblem of the joy inherent in football. Off the field, he embraced his role as a worldwide ambassador, bridging cultures via sport's common language.

The Flamboyant Swan Song of AC Milan

Ronaldinho's career took a new turn when he moved to AC Milan. While his flamboyance remained, his game had matured. Ronaldinho enriched his legacy by contributing to Milan's success, demonstrating that his magic was ageless, changing with time.

A Philanthropic Maestro Beyond Football

Ronaldinho's influence extended beyond stadiums. The man who created the ball danced with charities as well. From charity matches to humanitarian concerns, he used his celebrity to help people in need. Ronaldinho, the footballing virtuoso, has also come to represent kindness and charity.

A Footballing Odyssey of Difficulties and Resilience

Ronaldinho's path was not without difficulties. Off-field scandals and personal trials put his fortitude to the test. Despite the ups and downs, the enchantment in his boots never faded. Ronaldinho's ability to overcome hardship gave the icon more humanity, making him more relatable and admired.

The Smiles He Has Left Behind

Ronaldinho's influence extended beyond statistics and titles when the last whistle sounded on his spectacular career. He left a trail of smiles—those of spectators who watched his magic, opponents who admired his talent, and countless children who were encouraged to pick up a ball and dream.

WHAT DID WE LEARN FROM HIM?

Ronaldinho, the master of the beautiful game, tells us that football is an art form as well as a sport. His approach transcends competition, embracing the sport's intrinsic joy, innovation, and freedom. Ronaldinho's career exemplifies the transformational force of resilience, enthusiasm, and an unrelenting devotion to self-expression, from the dirt streets of Porto Alegre to the magnificent stages of Barcelona and beyond.

His ability to transform the football field into a canvas, painting with flicks, tricks, and hypnotic talents, shows us that greatness is about leaving an unforgettable impression on the hearts of fans all around the world, not simply goals. Beyond the confines of the stadium, Ronaldinho's generosity reminds us that sports personalities can be agents of positive change, utilizing their platform to help communities.

Ronaldinho's career, punctuated by highs and lows, teaches us about the human experience—overcoming obstacles, embracing joy in the face of hardship, and leaving a legacy that transcends statistics. In essence, Ronaldinho teaches that football is more than simply a game; it is a celebration of life, a dance with destiny, and an endless source of inspiration for future generations.

"I learned to play with joy, to love the game, always to have a smile on my face. This is what I really want from my players."

8

DIEGO MARADONA

"I am Maradona, who makes goals, who makes mistakes. I can take it all, I have shoulders big enough to fight with everybody."

DIEGO MARADONA: THE HAND OF GOD AND GENIUS' FEET

On October 30, 1960, a small child named Diego Armando Maradona was born in the midst of Villa Fiorito, a shantytown on the outskirts of Buenos Aires, Argentina. Little did the world realize that this destitute area would produce one of the greatest players in history, a man whose journey would be distinguished by amazing skill, victories, controversies, and a legacy that beyond the sport.

Starting in the Slums: The Streets that Made a Legend

Diego Maradona's youth was a far cry from the flash and splendor of his adult life. Growing up in poverty, he discovered his passion for football on the dusty alleys of Villa Fiorito. The ball became his buddy, and the obstacles of his neighborhood served as a training ground for a skill that would eventually enchant the world.

The Prodigy of Argentinos Juniors

Maradona made his professional debut for Argentinos Juniors at the age of 15. His rapid dribbling, close ball control, and daring approach propelled him to stardom. It didn't take long for the rest of the world to notice this small genius who seemed to dance with the ball at his feet.

Boca Juniors' Ascension to Stardom

Maradona's time with Boca Juniors pushed him into the Argentine football spotlight. He led Boca Juniors to the league title in 1981, demonstrating the type of individual brilliance that would become associated with his name. A footballing phenomena was on the rise across the world.

Barcelona Calling: The Rest of the World at His Feet

Maradona made a record-breaking move to Barcelona in 1982, becoming the most expensive player in the world. His stay in Spain was a flurry of success, controversy, and magical experiences. The world was introduced to Maradona's bold brilliance, who had an amazing ability to confuse defenders and awe crowds.

Mexico 1986: God's Hand and the Century's Goal

The 1986 World Cup in Mexico cemented Maradona's place in football history. His performances were nothing short of extraordinary. The iconic "Hand of God" goal, in which Maradona punched the ball into the net with his fist, was a controversial and audacious moment. However, it was his "Goal of the Century" against England in the same game that demonstrated his heavenly talent. Maradona dribbled past five English outfield players to score a game-changing goal.

From Rags to Riches: Napoli

The story of Maradona's time at Napoli is legendary. Maradona became a beacon of optimism in a community where economic woes loomed big. In 1987 and 1990, he guided Napoli to their first-ever Serie A triumphs, propelling the club to unparalleled heights. The people of Naples, who had faced adversity, discovered a hero in Maradona, a man capable of performing miracles on the field.

Struggles and Controversies Away from the Field

Off the pitch, Maradona's life was overshadowed by problems, including bouts with addiction and legal issues. His celebrity and the difficulties that came with it had an impact on his personal life. Despite these difficulties, Maradona's fortitude and ability to overcome hardship added dimensions to his complicated story.

Later Years: Managing and Motivating a Nation

Following his playing career, Maradona worked as a coach and manager. During the 2010 World Cup, he assumed command of the Argentine national team and, despite problems, left an indelible impact on a new generation of players. His ability to connect with and motivate his teammates paralleled his effect as a player.

More Than a Footballer's Legacy

Diego Maradona's influence reaches well beyond the football field. His influence on the game is evident, but it is his ability to transcend sports and become a cultural hero that distinguishes him. Maradona's legacy lives on in the hearts of all who witnessed his magic, from the fiery streets of Naples to the gigantic stadiums of the World Cup.

WHAT DID WE LEARN FROM HIM?

The biography of Diego Maradona tells us that greatness may emerge from the most unexpected places. His path from the impoverished neighborhoods of Villa Fiorito to the pinnacle of international football exemplifies the transformational power of talent, determination, and an unbreakable spirit. Maradona proved that football is more than simply a sport; he danced with the ball, creating a legacy of fascinating moments that transcend the game.

His ability to overcome hardship on and off the field exemplifies humanity's capacity for perseverance and redemption. Maradona's shortcomings and tribulations personalize his narrative, making it accessible to those experiencing similar difficulties. The contentious "Hand of God" event and the exquisite "Goal of the Century" show that even in the quest of greatness, flaws and genius coexist.

Maradona's influence extended beyond football into the cultural and social arenas, particularly in Naples, where he became a symbol of hope for a downtrodden society. His life teaches us about the complexities of celebrity, the weight of expectations, and the value of using one's power for good. In his entirety, Diego Maradona is a celebration of the beautiful game and the indomitable human spirit.

"When people succeed, it is because of hard work. Luck has nothing to do with success."

9

DAVID BECKHAM

"The only time you run out of chances is when you stop taking them."

BEYOND THE PITCH, BEYOND BORDERS: DAVID BECKHAM

On May 2, 1975, a legend was born amid the expansive suburbs of East London. In Leytonstone, David Robert Joseph Beckham, the man who would revolutionize football, flair, and worldwide renown, began his adventure. Little did the world realize that this ordinary youngster would grow into a remarkable figure, leaving an indelible impression not just on the football field, but also in fashion, philanthropy, and the entire notion of stardom.

Early Years: The Ball and the Dream

David Beckham's journey begins with modest origins. He was up in a middle-class family and inherited his father's passion for football. Beckham's career began with a ball, a dream, and an unwavering resolve to make his mark in the sport he loved, from the humble grounds of Ridgeway Rovers to the grandeur of Old Trafford.

Manchester United's Ascension to Superstardom

Beckham's exceptional talent drew the attention of Manchester United's legendary Class of '92 youth academy. Sir Alex Ferguson helped him develop into a swashbuckling midfielder with a talent for accurate free-kicks and unrivaled crossing skills. Beckham's talent was on display during United's treble-winning season in 1999, which paved the foundation for his stratospheric ascension to football superstardom.

Beyond Football: The Beckham Brand Soars

Beckham's dominance in the football world extended beyond the confines of the field. His marriage to Victoria Adams, called Posh Spice, launched him into famous royalty. They were the 'It' couple of the late '90s, appearing on magazine covers and red carpets. Beckham's chiseled features and growing sense of style established him as a fashion hero, opening the path for his entry into sponsorships and business.

A Global Icon Takes Center Stage at Galáctico in Madrid

Beckham began a new chapter in 2003, when he joined Real Madrid as part of the Galácticos period. His entrance in Madrid was not only a football transfer, but a seismic cultural event. Beckham's impact rose enormously off the field, cementing his stature as a global superstar. His time at Madrid demonstrated his ability to adapt not just to different footballing methods, but also to other cultures and expectations.

Hollywood Calling: The Bend It Like Beckham Phenomenon

The 2002 film "Bend It Like Beckham" popularized Beckham's name well beyond the footballing world. The film, which depicted a little girl's love of football and her idolization of David Beckham, became a cultural classic. The title of the film became synonymous with Beckham's amazing ability to curve the ball with accuracy, emphasizing his effect off the field.

Major League Soccer (MLS): A Cross-Continental Adventure

Beckham's choice to join the LA Galaxy in 2007 was a strategic one as much as a sports one. His entrance constituted a watershed moment in the history of Major League Soccer (MLS) in the United States. The "Beckham Effect" led to greater attendance, more media coverage, and increased interest in American soccer. Beyond the field, Beckham's entry into MLS paved the way for other foreign players to explore the league as a possible destination.

A Multifaceted Legacy of Paris, Fashion, and Philanthropy

Beckham's transfer to Paris Saint-Germain in 2013 was more than simply a move to further his football career; it was a statement of intent. He donated his full salary to a local children's charity, demonstrating a generous streak that has run through his life. Beckham's dedication to many charity initiatives, notably UNICEF, underlined his confidence in leveraging his celebrity to make a positive difference.

A New Chapter for the Beckhams in Miami

Beckham has now put his sights on a new frontier: football ownership. Beckham's move from the field to the boardroom is marked with the formation of Inter Miami CF, a Major League Soccer franchise. His ambition for the club extends beyond athletic achievement to include community participation, diversity, and the establishment of a lasting legacy in the lively city of Miami.

WHAT DID WE LEARN FROM HIM?

Determination Knows No Background:

Beckham's rise from a middle-class family in East London to a global icon proves that determination and talent can propel anyone beyond their circumstances.

Adaptability is Key to Longevity:

From Manchester to Madrid, and beyond, Beckham's ability to adapt, both on and off the pitch, underscores the importance of versatility in navigating the twists and turns of life.

Beyond Football: A Multidimensional Persona:

Beckham's success extends beyond his footballing prowess. His ventures in fashion, film, and philanthropy exemplify the possibility of a multidimensional career.

Impact Beyond Borders:

Whether in Manchester, Madrid, Los Angeles, or Miami, Beckham's influence has transcended geographical boundaries, proving that a global impact is achievable with the right vision.

Philanthropy as a Lifelong Commitment:

Beckham's dedication to charitable causes emphasizes the responsibility of individuals with influence to contribute positively to society.

"I want my children to see Daddy happy and passionate about work. And I want them to know that hard work pays off."

10

ZLATAN IBRAHIMOVIC

"I'm always looking forward. I don't dwell on things, I think about what's next."

ZLATAN IBRAHIMOVIC: THE FOOTBALL JUNGLE'S LION

On October 3, 1981, a kid named Zlatan Ibrahimovic was born in the Malmö suburbs of Sweden. From these humble beginnings sprang a footballing behemoth, a lion among men. Zlatan's journey is more than a football narrative; it's a monument to the tenacious spirit of a guy who cut his own way in the football jungle.

Early Years: The Sowing of Ambition

Adversity plagued Zlatan's youth. Growing up in Rosengrd, an immigrant-heavy region, he endured hardships that shaped his intense resolve. Football became his haven, a place where he could display the exceptional skill that distinguished him even at such a young age.

A Star is Born at Malmö FF

Zlatan's rise began with Malmö FF. Scouts took notice of his performances, and he soon found himself wearing the blue and gold shirt of Ajax. The world met a towering figure with an incredible knack for scoring and a flair for the extraordinary.

Ajax: Arrival in Grand Style

Zlatan's transfer to Ajax in 2001 signalled the start of his international adventure. His daring goals, notably a spectacular back-heel against NAC Breda, demonstrated not just skill but also a degree of confidence bordering on arrogance. Zlatan Ibrahimovic was the new mystery in the footballing world.

Juventus: Turin's Gigantic Titan

Zlatan Ibrahimovic joined Juventus in 2004, and the Turin fans witnessed the birth of a real footballing force. His collaboration with David Trezeguet was fearsome, and the goals came easily. However, the Calciopoli scandal loomed, and ultimately to Juventus' relegation.

Inter Milan's First Glimpse of European Glory

Zlatan's next stop was Inter Milan, when he first experienced the sweet nectar of Serie A victory. The collaboration with Jose Mourinho was legendary, and the Scudetto became a fixture at the San Siro. Zlatan's combination of strength, talent, and willpower made him a fan favourite.

Barcelona: Pep Guardiola's Titans clash

When Zlatan moved to Barcelona in 2009, he met Pep Guardiola, the tactical genius. The clash of egos resulted in a turbulent partnership, and Zlatan, despite his apparent brilliance, found himself looking for fresh opportunities.

AC Milan's Rossoneri Revival

Zlatan Ibrahimovic staged a resurgence in Italy, this time in the red and black of AC Milan. Zlatan Ibrahimovic's goals lifted Milan back into the Serie A debate, and his effect on and off the field was evident.

Paris Saint-Germain (PSG): Taking Control of the City of Light

Zlatan accepted a fresh challenge with PSG in 2012. The City of Light became his kingdom, and PSG established dominance in French football under his rule. Zlatan's ambitions and larger-than-life character made him a Parisian icon.

Manchester United: England's Lion Roars

The Premier League beckoned, and Zlatan accepted, joining Manchester United in 2016. Despite his late-career arrival, he had an instant effect, leading United to a Europa League victory and leaving an enduring influence on English football.

The Lion Roars Across the Atlantic for the LA Galaxy

Zlatan maintained his goal-scoring heroics in Major League Soccer after crossing the Atlantic to join the LA Galaxy in 2018. The lion had aged, but his roar was still as powerful as ever.

AC Milan Redux: The Prodigal Son Returns

Zlatan Ibrahimovic returns to AC Milan in 2020, overcoming both age and critics. His performances, highlighted by jaw-dropping goals and captain's impact, demonstrated the lion's ravenous desire for triumph.

A Captain's Legacy on the National Team

Zlatan's experience with the Swedish national team demonstrates his unwavering dedication. He led with a lion's heart from his early days until the end of his worldwide career, creating a legacy that inspired a generation.

Off the Field: The Lion's Mane Outside of Football

Zlatan's demeanor off the field is just as appealing as his on-field exploits. Zlatan's style matches his larger-than-life nature, with his lion's mane, tattoos, and swagger. Beyond the bravado lies a man with good business acumen, with enterprises in fashion and perfumes.

Zlatanisms: Zlatan's Wit and Wisdom

Zlatan's ability with words is famous, as are his goals. From calling himself a "Ferrari among Fiats" to saying, "I can't help but laugh at how perfect I am," Zlatan's self-assurance borders on the ridiculous. However, underneath the bluster is an underlying message: unashamedly believe in yourself.

Philanthropy: The Lion's Heart Contributes

Zlatan's charitable activities show a different side to the lion. He utilizes his success to improve others, from supporting charities to donating to needy areas, illustrating that even a lion has compassion for the less fortunate.

Injuries: The Lion's Fortitude

Injuries have marred Zlatan's career, including a possibly career-ending knee injury in 2017. Nonetheless, he battled back like a genuine lion, overcoming age and physical difficulties to continue roaring on the football field.

WHAT DID WE LEARN FROM HIM?

Through his incredible journey, Zlatan Ibrahimovic, the lion of football, provides vital lessons. His bravery in the face of adversity shows us that ambition has no limitations. Zlatan's adaptation, as seen by his smooth transfers between teams and nations, highlights the power found in flexibility and a readiness to take on new tasks.

As a captain with a lion's heart, Zlatan illustrates that genuine leadership needs bravery, persistence, and a dedication to leading by example. His acceptance of individuality inspires others to embrace their unique talents, building a society that values honesty.

Zlatan's age-defying exploits call into question conventional beliefs about the restrictions that come with becoming older. His tenacity in the face of adversity demonstrates the strength of desire to overcome adversity.

In summary, Zlatan Ibrahimovic shows us that success is a journey distinguished by daring, flexibility, leadership, individualism, and the unshakeable idea that age is simply a number in the quest of greatness. The lion's roar resonates as a reminder that with the appropriate mentality, any footballing jungle or life problem can be conquered.

"I have a winning mentality, and that's what I try to create at any club I go to. I am a lion, I am a predator. I want to win. I hate losing, and that mentality is what I will always try to instill in my teammates."

11

ANDRES INIESTA

"Respect is one of the most beautiful things in football."

ANDRÉS INIESTA: THE MAESTRO'S MIDFIELD MELODY

A little child named Andrés Iniesta began spinning a footballing tapestry that would dazzle audiences all over the world in the lovely village of Fuentealbilla, Spain. Iniesta's journey, which began on May 11, 1984, is one of midfield wizardry, crafted with grace, vision, and an instinctive knowledge of the beautiful game.

The Humble Beginnings of Fuentealbilla

Iniesta's love affair with football began on the dusty streets of Fuentealbilla, where he grew up in a close-knit neighborhood. The ball became an extension of his talent, and the small-town pitches served as the canvas for his early dazzling brushstrokes. Iniesta's path from Fuentealbilla to the global football arena was put in motion by his father's enthusiasm for the game.

From his early years, Iniesta's game was defined by precise ball control and exquisite passing. His youthful fantasies of greatness began to come true as he demonstrated a degree of technical competence that distinguished him. The echoes of his Fuentealbilla days would reverberate through Europe's major stadiums.

The Barça Ballet's La Masia Movement Begins

Iniesta's abilities drew the attention of FC Barcelona's La Masia youth program, which he enrolled at the age of 12. The Catalan club served as the canvas for Iniesta's footballing masterpiece. His ability to control the game's flow from midfield and his vision for breaking down defenses won him a berth on the first team.

The early 2000s saw the birth of the Barça Ballet, at which time Barcelona's tiki-taka style of play achieved its pinnacle. Along with Xavi Hernandez and Lionel Messi, Iniesta's smooth assimilation into the first squad created the backbone of a team that would revolutionize footballing aesthetics.

Crescendo El Clásico: Midfield Symphony

Iniesta's El Clásico performances versus Real Madrid become symphonies of midfield wizardry. His ability to pierce opposing defenses with clever dribbles and accurate passes made an indelible mark on football history. The midfield trio of Iniesta, Xavi, and Sergio Busquets became the beating core of Barcelona's success, coordinating domestic and international successes.

Overture to the World Cup: The Spanish Symphony

Iniesta led the Spanish national side to victory in the 2010 FIFA World Cup in South Africa. His extra-time winner in the final against the Netherlands cemented his place in Spanish football history. Iniesta's celebration, which included taking off his shirt to unveil a memorial to the late Dani Jarque, exemplified the emotional depth he brought to the game.

The World Cup victory capped a journey that began on the desolate lanes of Fuentealbilla. Iniesta's impact on the Spanish midfield, along with his ability to produce under duress, cemented his reputation as one of the finest midfielders of his generation.

Crescendo in the Champions League: European Elevation

Iniesta's performance in the UEFA Champions League paralleled his international success. His deft touches and incisive passes led Barcelona to several European titles. Iniesta's capacity to flourish on the biggest stage was seen in the 2009 and 2011 Champions League finals, both against Manchester United, winning him praise from fans and colleagues alike.

An Emotional Conclusion to Barcelona

After 22 years at Barcelona, Iniesta said an emotional farewell to the club where he became a famous in 2018. His departure signaled the end of an era, creating a gap that would be difficult to fill. Iniesta's impact extended beyond the pitch; he personified La Masia's principles and the spirit of Catalonia.

Oriental Harmonies: A J-League Journey

Iniesta made an unexpected transfer to the J-League, signing with Vissel Kobe in Japan. His presence added a touch of Spanish beauty to Japanese football. Iniesta continued to amaze with his on-field intellect and leadership, demonstrating that his footballing symphony could be heard around the globe.

Off the Field: A Gentleman's Behaviour

Iniesta's demeanor off the field complemented his grace on it. He won the affection of fans all around the world for his modesty and sportsmanship. Iniesta's dedication to fair play and respect for opponents enriched his already remarkable career.

Finally, the Maestro's Legacy

Andrés Iniesta's career is more than simply a list of achievements; it is a musical journey that has enhanced the world of football. His legacy is synonymous with football flair, intellect, and sportsmanship. Iniesta's journey exemplifies the ageless beauty of the game and the lasting influence of a real midfield master. As the echoes of his final whistle linger, Iniesta's legacy continues to inspire a new generation of football fans, reminding them that the true beauty of the game comes in its conductors' talent.

WHAT DID WE LEARN FROM HIM?

We take important insights from the maestro's journey as we conclude the symphony that is Andrés Iniesta's distinguished career. Iniesta, the personification of humility in greatness, illustrated that genuine winners are identified not just by their on-field talent but also by their constant modesty and respect. His knowledge of the complexities of football is a constant source of inspiration, underlining the significance of continual study and craftsmanship in the quest of perfection.

With the memorable World Cup-winning goal, Iniesta stamped his name in football legend, demonstrating the unbreakable spirit required of a real leader. His symbiotic teaming with luminaries like Lionel Messi illustrates the importance of collaboration and understanding on the field, demonstrating that brilliance is frequently a collaborative effort.

Iniesta's cultural influence and worldwide ambassador-ship have transcended boundaries, connecting followers in a common passion of the beautiful game. His impact goes far beyond prizes and honors, leaving an unforgettable imprint on the hearts of those who watched his symphony come to life. Andrés Iniesta's career is a tribute to the lasting strength of sportsman-ship, talent, and the creativity that characterizes the beautiful game in the broad fabric of football history.

"You can learn a lot from your teammates and your opponents, and you can always improve."

12

THIERRY HENRY

"I learned that if you want to make it bad enough, no matter how bad it is, you can make it."

THIERRY HENRY'S ELEGANCE AND TRIUMPH SYMPHONY

A little kid called Thierry Daniel Henry began a quest that would combine skill, elegance, and an unwavering drive to achieve in the busy suburbs of Les Ulis, France. Thierry's story, which began on August 17, 1977, is a symphony of footballing talent that resonates well beyond the fields he touched.

The Early Notes of Brilliance by Les Ulis

Growing up in a varied town, Henry's enthusiasm for football was sparked on the nearby Les Ulis fields. The ball became an extension of his imagination, and the streets served as the canvas for his first brilliant brushstrokes. Henry's path from Les Ulis to football success was sparked by his father's passion for the game.

Even in those early days, Henry's instinctive talent to maneuver past defenders and find the back of the net was clear. As he refined his abilities in the competitive environment of French youth football, his boyhood aspirations of grandeur began to reality. The echoes of his Les Ulis days would later ring in Europe's grandest stadiums.

The Monaco Movement: A Wave of Recognition

Henry's abilities piqued the interest of AS Monaco, where he made his professional debut at the age of 17. The Monaco chapter was a high point in the young striker's career. His scorching pace, precision finishing, and football intellect propelled him to the forefront of the French football scene.

The world experienced Henry's ability to lead from the front when he led Monaco to a surprising Ligue 1 triumph in 1996-97. His performances grabbed the attention of Europe's footballing elite, laying the groundwork for a transfer that would propel him to legendary status.

Arsenal Overture: A Red and White Symphony

Arsène Wenger created a masterpiece when he brought Thierry Henry to Arsenal in 1999. The transfer signaled the start of a new age in English football. Henry's on-field flair, characterized by balletic moves and a deadly scoring touch, captivated spectators and perplexed opponents.

Henry's orchestration of success was on display throughout the Invincibles' 2003-04 season. His 30 league goals were the keys to Arsenal's undefeated season. As he proceeded to produce footballing poetry in the famous red and white shirt, Henry's Premier League Golden Boot became a frequent presence on his mantle.

Barcelona Ballad: Ascending to New Heights

Henry joined a new movement in 2007, joining Barcelona. The Blaugrana Symphony Orchestra, led by maestro Pep Guardiola, welcomed Henry. Henry participated to a treble-winning season in 2008-09 alongside Lionel Messi and Samuel Eto'o.

Barcelona's playing style, defined by rapid, complex passes and fluid moves, matched Henry's delicacy well. Henry lifted the UEFA Champions League trophy in the final, capping off an incredible European career. His stay at Barcelona cemented his place as a global football legend.

Note from New York: The MLS Sonata

As the European chapters of his career came to an end, Henry moved to Major League Soccer (MLS) with the New York Red Bulls. His influence grew beyond the pitch as he accepted the position of mentor and leader. The MLS observed Henry's ability to score goals and play well, demonstrating that his footballing symphony recognized no geographical boundaries.

National Harmony: Les Bleus Symphony

The international career of Thierry Henry with the French national team has been a symphony of highs and lows. Henry's passion to Les Bleus represented a genuine link with national pride, from winning the 1998 FIFA World Cup on home soil to the anguish of the 2006 final. His goal-scoring prowess for France is inextricably linked to the country's footballing heritage.

The Montreal Movement: A Farewell Crescendo

In his final playing move, Henry became head coach of the Montreal Impact. This change represented his determination to give back to the sport that had given him so much. The Impact resurrected under Henry's leadership, combining his tactical knowledge with the enthusiasm he demonstrated on the field.

Philanthropic Harmony: Off the Pitch

Aside from his charitable initiatives, Henry's legacy includes a humanitarian note. Henry's devotion to having a good influence off the field demonstrates the depth of his character, from efforts assisting needy communities to pushing for social justice.

WHAT DID WE LEARN FROM HIM?

Thierry Henry, a football virtuoso of unrivaled finesse, delivers timeless principles that extend beyond the bounds of the beautiful game. Henry illustrates us the strength of perseverance in pursuing one's goal, from his early days in Les Ulis to the major stages of international football. His path demonstrates that success is defined by the grace and efficiency with which it is attained.

Henry's leadership, both as club and country captain, acts as a light for aspiring leaders, demonstrating that genuine leadership goes beyond wearing the armband and focuses on motivating and uplifting people around you. His global success highlights football's international language, reminding us of the sport's capacity to connect disparate cultures and communities.

Above all, Thierry Henry's life committed to football, smoothly shifting from player to coach, illustrates that the sport is a way of life, not simply a vocation. His long reputation mirrors the ideas that a great footballing legend is defined by quality, elegance, and an uncompromising devotion to one's trade. Henry's story is a masterpiece in the art of football, leaving us with lasting marks of the game's eternal fascination.

"You have to believe in yourself when no one else does – that makes you a winner right there."

13

NEYMAR

"My motivation has always been to play football and to be happy. I don't need to show anyone or prove anything."

NEYMAR: A SKILL AND RESILIENCE SAMBA SYMPHONY

A little child called Neymar do Silva Santos Jnior began a path that would redefine football creativity in the lively neighborhoods of Mogi das Cruzes, Brazil. Neymar's journey, which began on February 5, 1992, is a samba symphony of skill, resilience, and a never-ending quest of perfection.

The Beginnings of the Favela: Fanning the Flame

Growing up in the Praia Grande area of Rio de Janeiro, Neymar's passion for football shone through even in the face of adversity. His training grounds were the makeshift fields of the favelas, and the ball became an extension of his spirit. Neymar Santos Sr., his father, saw his son's natural potential and became a guiding force in supporting the young prodigy's aspirations.

Neymar's natural ability to control the ball with ease and perform daring movements set him unique from an early age. Neymar's father, a former player, mentored him, emphasizing discipline and determination in his approach to the game. Neymar's early talent was nurtured amid the dusty alleys of Praia Grande, where he polished the abilities that would eventually enchant the footballing world.

The Prodigy's Stage at Santos FC

Neymar joined the Santos FC junior club at the age of 11, where his flair and imagination instantly distinguished him. His impressive displays for Santos' senior team heralded the arrival of a footballing prodigy. Neymar enthralled fans with his ability to waltz past defenders with the ball at his feet and score with flair, and he guided Santos to multiple trophies, including the Copa Libertadores in 2011.

Neymar's time at Santos FC was a triumph of brilliance. His collaboration with another young star, Ganso, created plays that reflected the beauty of Brazil's footballing heritage. Neymar's daring on the ball, along with his goal-scoring ability, earned him a fan favorite at Santos. When he won the renowned South American Footballer of the Year award in 2011, the world took notice.

Barcelona Ballet: The European Journey

Neymar moved to Barcelona in 2013, when he joined forces with Lionel Messi and Andrés Iniesta. The trio captivated the globe with their sophisticated play, becoming a footballing trifecta. Neymar's contribution to Barcelona's treble-winning season in 2014-2015 cemented his status among the world's top.

Neymar's move to Barcelona constituted a watershed moment in his career. Playing alongside Messi, widely considered as one of the best footballers of all time, was a challenge as well as a chance. Neymar's versatility and eagerness to learn, on the other hand, helped him to smoothly blend into the Barcelona team.

Messi, Neymar, and Luis Suárez, known together as "MSN," became associated with offensive prowess. The combination between Neymar and Messi, in particular, demonstrated telepathic understanding on the field. The fabled trio guided Barcelona to domestic and international glory, with Neymar's flair and goal-scoring skill bringing a new layer of excitement to the team's play.

The PSG Era in Parisian Dreams

Neymar's record-breaking move to Paris Saint-Germain (PSG) in 2017 signaled the beginning of a new chapter in his career. Despite adversity and injury, he maintained his footballing prowess, establishing lethal combinations with Kylian Mbappé and Edinson

Cavani. Neymar was instrumental in PSG's domestic and international triumphs.

The transfer to PSG was more than just a transfer; it was a declaration of purpose. Neymar was looking for fresh challenges and the chance to lead a club to European triumph. Despite being absent by injury at critical times, Neymar's effect on PSG's offense was apparent. His relationship with Mbappé and Cavani produced a trident that frightened rival defenders and helped Paris Saint-Germain win several domestic titles.

Seleço Brava: National Pride

Neymar's international career has been a rollercoaster ride while wearing Brazil's famed yellow shirt. Neymar's commitment to representing his nation has been consistent, from winning the FIFA Confederations Cup in 2013 to suffering heartbreak in the 2014 World Cup. His perseverance in the face of adversity demonstrates a resolve to bring honor to Brazil.

The weight of a nation's expectations rests on Neymar's shoulders as Brazil's star. The highs of big tournament victories are offset by the lows of injuries and near misses. Neymar's finest moment was expected to be the 2014 World Cup on home soil, but an injury in the semifinals crushed those ambitions. Nonetheless, his love for the yellow jersey and dedication to the Brazilian cause continue, making him a national figure.

Away from the Pitch: The Philanthropist

Beyond the glitz of the game, Neymar is an active philanthropist. His charity endeavors, such as the Instituto Neymar Jr., show his dedication to bettering the lives of impoverished youngsters in Brazil.

Neymar's charitable efforts mirror his personal path. The Instituto Neymar Jr. was founded in 2014 with the goal of offering educational and recreational possibilities for youngsters in Praia Grande and beyond. Neymar's dedication to giving back to his community displays a great appreciation for the possibilities football has provided him.

The Neymar Story: Obstacles and Triumphs

From on-field skirmishes to relentless monitoring of his lifestyle, Neymar's path has not been without controversy. These difficulties, however, have just fueled his resolve to prove himself time and again.

On and off the field, Neymar has faced criticism. His playing style, which is marked by flair and theatrics, has sparked discussion. Nonetheless, Neymar's answer has been to let his game speak for itself. He has repeatedly silenced his detractors with goals, assists, and flashes of brilliance.

Injuries have been another stumbling block in Neymar's journey. Injuries have put his endurance to the test, from vital periods in club contests to pivotal junctures in international games. Nonetheless, he has recovered each time, displaying the mental toughness that distinguishes the game's greats.

Legacy: The Neymar Story Continues

Neymar's impact goes beyond goals and trophies as he continues to weave his tale on the world football stage. Neymar's story is one of skill, perseverance, and the sheer joy that football offers. Neymar da Silva Santos Jnior adds a new note to the samba symphony of football with each step, dribble, and goal, leaving a legacy that will be felt for centuries.

The Artistry of Neymar's Influence on Football

Neymar's impact on the beautiful game goes beyond numbers. His playing style is an artistic expression, a blend of talent, flair, and inventiveness that takes football to the level of an art form. Neymar delivers a particular type of entertainment to the pitch, whether it's a subtle move, a crisp pass, or a dazzling goal celebration.

The significance of the Brazilian striker goes beyond the pitch, influencing how football is regarded and celebrated. His charm, both on and off the field, has turned him into a global phenomenon, drawing followers from all over the world. The Neymar brand is more than just a player; it represents a way of life, an attitude, and an uncompromising devotion to self-expression.

Neymar is a global icon.

Neymar's rise from the Brazilian favelas to the pinnacle of European and international football reflects the sport's global character. His popularity crosses borders, making him a cultural phenomenon and a source of motivation for young football players all across the world.

The Neymar story is still evolving, with more chapters to come. Neymar remains an ever-evolving force in football as he continues to captivate spectators with his skill, passion, and love for the game. Neymar's narrative is a monument to the eternal enchantment of the beautiful game, from the dirt alleyways of Mogi das Cruzes to the great stages of the UEFA Champions League.

WHAT DID WE LEARN FROM HIM?

Neymar, the Brazilian soccer virtuoso, has left an ever-lasting imprint on the beautiful game. Neymar teaches numerous vital lessons with his spectacular footwork, flair, and goal-scoring skill. To begin, he teaches us the skill of creativity and expression on the pitch, reminding ambitious players that soccer is a canvas for individual talent rather than merely a sport.

Second, Neymar's mental fortitude is demonstrated by his resilience in the face of adversity. He illustrates the need of tenacity and mental strength in the pursuit of excellence, from surviving injuries to handling the challenges of worldwide popularity.

Neymar also emphasizes the importance of collaboration and friendship. His flawless collaborations with teammates demonstrate the value of teamwork, confirming that success in soccer is a communal effort rather than an individual one.

Off the field, Neymar's charity efforts emphasize the responsibility that comes with celebrity. He urges young fans to utilize their power constructively and have a real difference beyond the bounds of the soccer pitch through programs that provide educational opportunities and help to needy areas.

Neymar's narrative is essentially one of skill, resilience, teamwork, and social responsibility. Young fans who follow his journey learn not just soccer skills, but also life lessons that go beyond the confines of the sport.

"I've always tried to do my very best, and I want to keep doing that. I'm going to do everything I can to make people happy, to achieve my dreams, and to make a difference in the world."

14

RONALDO NAZARIO

"In football, as in life, you need to have a plan, stay focused, and never underestimate the power of resilience."

RONALDO NAZÁRIO: THE PHENOMENON'S RESILIENCE AND GLORY JOURNEY

A little child named Ronaldo Lus Nazário de Lima began a path that would redefine football glory in the lively neighborhoods of Bento Ribeiro, Rio de Janeiro. Ronaldo's narrative, which began on September 18, 1976, is one of raw talent, persistence, and an unshakable desire to overcome hardship.

Prelude by Bento Ribeiro: The Favela's Prodigy

Ronaldo's passion for football was kindled on the dusty streets of Bento Ribeiro, where he grew up. The ball became an extension of his aspirations, and the favela's improvised pitches served as testing grounds for his exceptional abilities. Ronaldo's natural ability to score goals, even as a boy, foreshadowed the extraordinary skill that would enchant the world.

Cruzeiro Crescendo: Brazil's Superstar

Ronaldo's abilities drew the attention of scouts, and at the age of 16, he joined Cruzeiro, kicking off a spectacular career. His accomplishments in Brazil piqued the interest of European powerhouses, and in 1996, Ronaldo moved to Europe to play for FC Barcelona.

The Blaugrana Symphony is a work of genius by Barça.

Ronaldo's talent reached new heights in Barcelona. His fast pace, precision finishing, and daring dribbling drew attention, giving him the moniker "The Phenomenon." Ronaldo's time at Barcelona was a symphony of goals, and he rapidly established himself as one of the world's most feared attackers.

Interlude at Inter: The Unveiling of Italian Opera

Ronaldo resumed his trip to Italy, where he joined Inter Milan. Despite suffering setbacks due to injury, Ronaldo shown tremendous fortitude. His remarkable recovery from a career-threatening knee injury demonstrated both his physical and emotional toughness.

Brazilian Glory beckons in the World Cup Overture

Ronaldo's career culminated on the largest platform of all: the FIFA World Cup. Ronaldo was ready to lead Brazil to gold in 1998, but a sad injury in the final put an end to the dream. However, Ronaldo's unbreakable spirit triumphed, and in 2002, he led Brazil to World Cup victory, cementing his position in football history.

Rhapsody of Real Madrid: The Galácticos Era

Ronaldo's adventure continued at Real Madrid, where he became part of the legendary Galácticos period. His goal-scoring exploits, as well as his collaboration with Zinedine Zidane and Raul, produced a footballing symphony. Ronaldo's reputation was characterized by his ability to enhance his game on the biggest stages.

Interlude by AC Milan: The Italian Encore

Ronaldo's stay in Italy was extended with AC Milan, adding another chapter to his illustrious career. His efforts to the Rossoneri cemented his standing as a footballing legend.

A Homecoming Swan Song: Corinthians Cadence

Ronaldo returned to Brazil in a poetic twist, signing with Corinthians. Despite his injuries, he showed glimpses of brilliance, leaving a lasting impression on the team and the fans who had admired him since infancy.

Humanitarian Harmony Off the Pitch

Ronaldo Nazário's effect stretched beyond the goals and the fame. His charitable endeavors, which included education and healthcare programs, demonstrated his dedication to make a good influence in the lives of others.

Conclusion: The Legacy of the Phenomenon

Ronaldo Nazário's journey is more than a symphony of wins, setbacks, and unshakable persistence. Ronaldo's career represents the universal strength of resilience and the quest of greatness, from the favelas of Rio to the major stages of European football. As the last whistle blows, Ronaldo Nazário's legacy lives on, encouraging future generations to think that they, too, can become footballing phenomenons with skill, tenacity, and a touch of magic.

WHAT DID WE LEARN FROM HIM?

Ronaldo Nazário exemplifies the persistent quest of excellence and an unbreakable spirit of perseverance. His story, distinguished by explosive skill and dramatic comebacks, shows us the value of overcoming hardship. Ronaldo's ability to overcome career-threatening injuries and disappointments demonstrates the value of mental toughness. Furthermore, his influence goes beyond the field, highlighting the importance of football icons as positive change ambassadors through philanthropy. Ronaldo Nazário's tale exemplifies the belief that genuine excellence overcomes adversity, and that failures are not the end, but rather an opportunity for a stunning return. His legacy inspires young footballers and fans alike, demonstrating that with persistence, enthusiasm, and an uncompromising devotion to one's objectives, the route to achievement can be just as spectacular as the destination.

"I learned that challenges are what make life interesting, and overcoming them is what makes life meaningful."

15

ROBERTO BAGGIO

I believe to have shown that, at times, the impossible can become possible. It all depends on how much each and every one of us believes in our dreams, in our strength, and in our determination.

ROBERTO BAGGIO'S JOURNEY OF GRACE AND REDEMPTION AS IL DIVIN CODINO

A little child named Roberto Baggio developed his love for football among the vineyards and cobblestone alleyways of Caldogno, Italy. Baggio's path from a modest hamlet to become one of football's most legendary players, born on February 18, 1967, is one of brilliance, tenacity, and the desire of atonement.

Caldogno Crescendo: The Beginnings of Brilliance

Baggio's love of the ball was obvious from an early age in the small alleys of Caldogno. His quick feet and natural football knowledge set him apart, attracting the attention of local scouts. At the age of 13, he joined Vicenza, starting a career that would cement his place in football history.

Vicenza Virtuoso: Il Divin Codino's Ascension

Baggio's time in Vicenza was a symphony of young zeal and blossoming skill. His talents drew the attention of bigger teams, resulting in a transfer to Fiorentina in 1985. Baggio's entrance in Florence heralded the birth of "Il Divin Codino" - The Divine Ponytail, a moniker that would reverberate through stadiums for years to come.

Fiorentina Flourish: Purple Jersey Artistry

Baggio's talents bloomed in the purple shirt of Fiorentina. Fans adored him for his spectacular runs, precision free kicks, and graceful playmaking. Despite the club's financial difficulties, Baggio's efforts inspired others, earning him the prized Ballon d'Or in 1993.

Turin Trials and Triumphs at Juventus Junction

Baggio's contentious transfer to Juventus in 1990 saw him assume the Old Lady's black and white stripes. Despite initial mistrust, he silenced detractors with outstanding performances, leading Juventus to Serie A championships. His influence was immense, and his superb musicianship continued to fascinate.

World Cup Disasters and Miracles: USA '94 Drama

Baggio's international career culminated at the 1994 FIFA World Cup, which was hosted in the United

States. Despite injuries, Baggio's performances pushed Italy to the final. The pivotal moment, however, came in the penalty shootout, when Baggio's blunder gave Brazil the win. The picture of Baggio in tears became an indelible part of the emotional fabric that is football.

Sojourn of AC Milan: Redemption and Rebirth

Baggio found salvation after joining AC Milan in 1995. He was instrumental in Milan's triumph, demonstrating not just his persistent talent but also his capacity to overcome adversity. Baggio's stay at Milan was another chapter in his illustrious career.

Swan Song by the Bologna Ballet in Rossoblù

Baggio joined Bologna in the twilight of his career, where he continued to show flashes of brilliance. His devotion to the game and desire to entertaining fans remained steadfast, solidifying his place as one of football's most lasting heroes.

Zen and Philanthropy Beyond Football

Baggio pursued Buddhist philosophy after retiring, finding peace in meditation and spirituality. His path took a charitable turn when he was appointed as a United Nations Goodwill Ambassador, where he used his position to fight for humanitarian concerns.

Conclusion: Il Divin Codino's Legacy

Roberto Baggio's legacy goes beyond the fields he played on. His is a narrative of perseverance, atonement, and the unwavering pursuit of perfection. Not only did Il Divin Codino leave an indelible impression on Italian football, but he also became a global emblem of grace and talent. Roberto Baggio's path exemplifies the transformational power of sport, demonstrating that even in the face of adversity, one may emerge as a renowned person, leaving behind a legacy that transcends time and turf.

WHAT DID WE LEARN FROM HIM?

We can learn a lot from Roberto Baggio about resilience, atonement, and the never-ending quest of perfection. His triumphant and tribulations-filled path shows us that setbacks are not the end, but rather possibilities for great comebacks. Baggio's ability to manage his career's highs and lows, from the peak of achievement to the depths of a missed penalty in a World Cup final, shows the strength found in vulnerability.

The narrative of Il Divin Codino also highlights the transforming effect of sport outside of the playing field. Baggio's exploration of Buddhist philosophy and later work as a UN Goodwill Ambassador demonstrate a dedication to personal development and making a positive effect on the world.

Baggio exemplifies the spirit of resilience in every twist of his career, reminding us that genuine greatness comes not just in one's triumphs, but also in how one rises to adversities. His influence goes far beyond sports, leaving us with a timeless pattern for dealing with hardship gracefully and emerging stronger on the other side.

"Football, for me, is an infinite passion that will always be around."

CONCLUSION

The stories of these great sportsmen serve as beacons of inspiration in the magnificent fabric of soccer, illuminating the route for young dreamers who dare to follow a ball and a vision. As the tales of this book come to a conclusion, the booming echo is one of triumph over hardship, of commitment that transcends the pitch, and of tenacious souls whose names will be etched in the annals of athletic history.

These soccer masters' stories are more than just goals and triumphs; they are sagas of tenacity, hard effort, and the never-ending quest of perfection. These athletes remind us that success is a path distinguished by discipline, passion, and unshakable devotion via the perspiration on their brows and delight in their successes.

For the young fans reading these pages, may the stories of Pelé, Messi, Ronaldo, Maradona, and others inspire them to pursue their aspirations. Aside from the sparkling goals and trophies, these players show that the path to success is littered with disappointments, and the capacity to emerge from defeat characterizes a great winner.

Aspiring sportsmen, both on and off the field, can take inspiration from these superstars' passion. Whether it's Pelé's renowned bicycle kicks, Messi's hypnotic dribbles, or Ronaldo's devastating strikes, each move is a monument to the endless hours of work, sacrifices made, and perseverance in the face of adversity.

This book is more than a soccer celebration; it's a life playbook. The concepts of discipline, collaboration, and tenacity that resound throughout these stories transcend sports, providing significant lessons for the young brains absorbing the wisdom contained inside these pages. These players inspire not just with their abilities but also with their spirit, from the muddy fields where dreams take root to the big stadiums where they flourish.

May the echoes of these stories of success continue, encouraging the next generation to lace up their boots, dream big, and grasp that the pursuit of perfection is more than simply a game—it's a way of life. May kids find encouragement to conquer their own fields, whether they are made of grass or aspirations, with every kick, sprint, and goal. These soccer legends' legacies linger on, handing the torch of inspiration to young hearts and minds ready to write their own triumphant stories.

Made in United States
Orlando, FL
12 October 2024

52482161R00072